EDMONDS
CHRISTMAS TREATS

EDMONDS
CHRISTMAS TREATS

Hodder Moa Beckett

CONTENTS

INTRODUCTION

Welcome to the third title in the new range of Edmonds 'mini' titles. Since 1907, Edmonds has helped many New Zealand cooks produce wonderful, tasty treats for family and friends alike. This tradition continues with these new books which explore individual styles of baking and cooking.

Christmas Treats expands on the foods for the festive season already provided in the baking section of the original *Edmonds Cookery Book*. *Christmas Treats* contains both traditional Edmonds recipes and a number of new recipes that allow the cook to produce tempting treats for your family Christmas.

Mouth-watering photography accompanies the recipes – and we certainly hope these tempt you to try all the recipes in the book.

We would love to hear your comments on this new title in the Edmonds range, so feel free to write to Bluebird Foods Limited, Private Bag, Manukau City, Auckland.

From all the Edmonds team, we wish you many hours of great baking and enjoyment over the festive season.

RICH CHRISTMAS CAKE

¾ cup dark rum or brandy

1¾ cups orange juice

2 tablespoons grated orange zest

500 g currants

500 g raisins

400 g sultanas

2 cups chopped dates

150 g crystallised ginger, chopped

150 g packet mixed peel

150 g packet glacé cherries, halved

½ teaspoon vanilla essence

¼ teaspoon almond essence

2 teaspoons grated lemon zest

1 cup blanched almonds

2½ cups Champion high grade flour

½ teaspoon Edmonds baking soda

1 teaspoon cinnamon

1 teaspoon mixed spice

½ teaspoon ground nutmeg

250 g butter, softened

1½ cups brown sugar

2 tablespoons treacle

5 eggs

GLAZE and DECORATION

¼ cup apricot jam

1 teaspoon gelatine

1 tablespoon cold water

halved cherries, halved dried apricots

blanched almonds

In a saucepan, bring to boil rum, orange juice and zest. Remove from heat. Add dried fruit. Cover and leave overnight. Stir essences, lemon zest and almonds into saucepan. Sift flour, soda and spices into a bowl. In another bowl, cream butter, sugar and treacle until light and fluffy. Add eggs one at a time, beating well after each egg. Fold in sifted ingredients alternately with fruit mixture. Line a deep, square 23 cm tin with two layers of brown paper then one layer of baking paper. Spoon mixture into tin. Bake at 150°C for 4 hours or until an inserted skewer comes out clean when tested. Cover tin with a piece of brown paper for first 2 hours of cooking to prevent top from browning too quickly. Leave in tin until cold. To glaze and decorate: Make glaze by melting jam. Push through a fine sieve. Sprinkle gelatine over cold water. Sit over bowl of hot water and stir until gelatine dissolves. Stir into jam. Brush top of cake with half the glaze. Arrange dried fruit and nuts. Brush with remaining glaze. Allow to set before wrapping in foil. Store in a cool place.

FESTIVE CHOCOLATE RUM CAKE

125 g butter, softened
¾ cup caster sugar
2 eggs
1¾ cups Champion standard
grade flour
½ cup cocoa
1 teaspoon Edmonds baking powder
1 teaspoon Edmonds baking soda
¾ cup warm milk
3 teaspoons instant coffee powder

¼ cup rum

GANACHE
150 g dark chocolate, chopped
(or melts or bits)
¼ cup cream

whipped cream and chocolate
shapes to garnish
icing sugar to dust

Cream butter and sugar until light and fluffy. Add eggs one at a time, beating well after each addition. Sift flour, cocoa and baking powder. Dissolve baking soda in milk, then whisk in coffee and rum. Fold dry ingredients and milk mixture alternately into butter mixture. Spoon into a greased 20 cm round cake tin that has been lined with baking paper on the base. Bake at 180°C for 45 minutes or until a skewer inserted in the centre of the cake comes out clean. Cool in tin for 10 minutes before transferring to a wire rack. When cold, cut cake horizontally into 3 equal portions. Place one portion on a serving plate and spread with half the ganache. Top with second portion and spread with remaining ganache. Place final portion of cake on top. To make the ganache, place chocolate and cream in a small saucepan. Stir over a low heat until chocolate melts and mixture is smooth. To serve, cut into wedges. Garnish with whipped cream and chocolate shapes. Dust with icing sugar.

CHOCOLATE SHAPES
Draw desired shapes onto baking paper. Pipe melted chocolate to outline. Randomly pipe lines inside shapes. Leave to set before removing from the paper.

LIGHT FRUIT CAKE

675 g mixed fruit

¼ cup mixed peel

2 tablespoons Champion high grade flour

¼ cup brandy or dark rum

225 g butter

1 cup brown sugar

2 tablespoons golden syrup

1 tablespoon marmalade

3 cups Champion high grade flour

1 teaspoon Edmonds baking powder

pinch of salt

1 teaspoon mixed spice

½ teaspoon ground nutmeg

5 eggs, beaten

Combine mixed fruit and peel in a bowl. Dust with the first measure of flour. Add brandy and mix well. Cream butter, sugar and golden syrup until light and fluffy. Stir in marmalade. Sift the second measure of flour, baking powder, salt, mixed spice and nutmeg together. Add flour and eggs alternately to creamed mixture. Add prepared fruit and mix well. Line a deep, 20 cm-square cake tin with two layers of brown paper followed by one layer of baking paper. Spoon mixture into cake tin, smoothing the surface. Bake at 150°C for 2–2½ hours or until an inserted skewer comes out clean. Leave in tin until cold. If desired, ice cake.

BOILED FRUIT CAKE

500 g mixed fruit
water
250 g butter, chopped
1½ cups sugar
3 eggs, beaten

3 cups Champion standard
grade flour
4 teaspoons Edmonds
baking powder
½ teaspoon almond essence
½ teaspoon vanilla essence

Put mixed fruit in a saucepan. Add just enough water to cover fruit. Cover and bring to the boil. Remove from heat. Stir in butter and sugar, stirring constantly until butter has melted. Allow to cool. Beat in eggs. Sift flour and baking powder into fruit mixture, stirring to combine. Stir in essences. Line a 24 cm round cake tin with two layers of brown paper followed by one layer of baking paper. Spoon mixture into cake tin. Bake at 160°C for 1½–2 hours or until an inserted skewer comes out clean. Leave in tin for 10 minutes before turning out onto a wire rack.

CATHEDRAL LOAF

125 g glacé pineapple rings
3 glacé pears
⅓ cup glacé green cherries
½ cup glacé red cherries
125 g glacé apricots
125 g blanched almonds
250 g whole brazil nuts
½ cup crystallised ginger
3 eggs

½ cup caster sugar
1 teaspoon vanilla essence
2 tablespoons brandy
¾ cup Champion standard
grade flour
½ teaspoon Edmonds
baking powder
1 teaspoon ground nutmeg
¼ teaspoon salt

Chop pineapple rings and pears into 6 pieces. Halve green and red cherries. Chop apricots into quarters. Put chopped fruits, almonds, brazil nuts and ginger into a bowl. Mix to combine. In a separate bowl beat eggs, sugar, essence and brandy together. Sift flour, baking powder, nutmeg and salt together. Fold sifted ingredients into egg mixture. Pour onto fruit and nuts, mixing thoroughly. Line a 23 cm loaf tin with two layers of brown paper followed by one layer of baking paper. Pour mixture into loaf tin. Bake at 150°C for 2 hours or until an inserted skewer comes out clean. Allow to cool in tin. Remove paper and wrap in foil to store. Leave for 2 days before cutting. To serve, use a sharp knife to cut into thin slices.

CASSATA

1 litre chocolate ice cream
½ teaspoon vanilla essence
500 ml vanilla ice cream
½ cup toasted slivered almonds
½ cup chopped dark chocolate
1 cup chopped glacé fruit (eg. papaya, apricots, pineapple)
melon balls to garnish (optional)

Soften chocolate ice cream and mix in essence. Use to line the base and sides of a 1 litre pudding basin. Freeze until firm. Soften vanilla ice cream. Fold in almonds, chocolate and glacé fruit. Use to fill the chocolate ice cream cavity. Cover with foil and freeze until firm. Unmould onto a serving plate by dipping bowl into hot water 2–3 times, then inverting onto a plate and shaking sharply. Cut into wedges to serve. Garnish with melon balls.
Serves 6–8.

CHOCOLATE ÉCLAIRS

100 g butter
1 cup water
1 cup Champion standard
grade flour
3 eggs
whipped cream

CHOCOLATE ICING
2 cups icing sugar
2 tablespoons cocoa
¼ teaspoon butter
¼ teaspoon vanilla essence
2 tablespoons boiling
water, approx.

Combine butter and water in a saucepan. Bring to a rolling boil. Remove from heat and quickly add flour. Beat with a wooden spoon until mixture leaves the sides of the saucepan. Allow to cool for 5 minutes. Add eggs one at a time, beating well after each addition, until mixture is glossy. Pipe 7 cm strips of the mixture onto greased oven trays. Bake at 200°C for 30 minutes or until éclairs are puffy and golden, then lower heat to 120°C and continue baking for about 15 minutes until dry. Cool thoroughly. Using a sharp knife, cut slits into the sides of each éclair. Fill with whipped cream and ice tops with Chocolate Icing. To make the Chocolate Icing, sift icing sugar and cocoa into a bowl. Add butter and essence. Add sufficient boiling water to mix to a spreadable consistency.
Makes 30.

CREAM PUFFS

Pipe or spoon heaped teaspoons of Chocolate Éclair mixture onto greased oven trays. Bake as above. Cool thoroughly. Fill with whipped cream and strawberries. Dust with icing sugar.

Chocolate Liqueur Mousse (Top left)
Chocolate Log (Top right)
Chocolate Éclairs (Cream Puff variation) (Bottom)

CHOCOLATE LIQUEUR MOUSSE

200 g cooking chocolate
3 eggs
¼ cup sugar
1 tablespoon brandy, chocolate or coffee liqueur
300 ml cream, whipped
whipped cream to garnish
flaked or grated chocolate to garnish

Break chocolate into the top of a double boiler. Stir over hot water until chocolate has melted. Allow to cool slightly. Using an electric mixer, beat eggs and sugar for about 5 minutes, until thick and pale. Add chocolate and beat until just combined. Using a large metal spoon, fold in brandy and whipped cream. Pour into six individual dishes or one large dish. Chill until firm. Decorate with whipped cream and chocolate. Serves 6.

CHOCOLATE LOG

3 eggs
½ cup sugar
½ teaspoon vanilla essence
2 tablespoons cocoa
¼ cup Champion standard
grade flour
1 teaspoon Edmonds
baking powder

25 g butter, melted
1 tablespoon water
icing sugar
raspberry jam
whipped cream

CHOCOLATE ICING
(see page 19)

Beat eggs, sugar and essence until thick and pale. Sift cocoa, flour and baking powder together. Fold into egg mixture then fold in butter and water. Pour mixture evenly over the base of a 20 x 30 cm sponge roll tin lined on the base with baking paper. Bake at 190°C for 10–12 minutes or until cake springs back when lightly touched. When cooked turn onto baking paper sprinkled with sifted icing sugar. Spread with jam and roll from the short side immediately, using the paper to help. Leave the roll wrapped in the paper until cold, then unroll, fill with whipped cream and re-roll gently. Ice with Chocolate Icing.

CHRISTMAS PUDDING

1 cup sultanas

1 cup raisins

1 cup currants

70 g packet blanched
almonds, chopped

150 g packet mixed peel

1 cup shredded suet

1 cup Champion standard grade flour

1½ teaspoons Edmonds
baking powder

1 teaspoon mixed spice

1 teaspoon cinnamon

¼ teaspoon ground nutmeg

¼ teaspoon salt

1½ cups soft breadcrumbs

1 cup brown sugar

2 eggs

2 teaspoons grated lemon zest

½ cup milk

1 tablespoon brandy

Put sultanas, raisins, currants, almonds and mixed peel into a large bowl. Add suet, mixing to combine. Sift flour, baking powder, mixed spice, cinnamon, nutmeg and salt into fruit mixture. Stir well. Add breadcrumbs and mix through. In a separate bowl, beat brown sugar, eggs, lemon zest and milk together. Add to fruit mixture, mixing thoroughly to combine. Stir in brandy. Spoon mixture into a well-greased 6-cup-capacity pudding basin. Cover with pleated greaseproof paper or foil. Secure with string, leaving a loop to lift out pudding when cooked. Place a trivet or old saucer in the bottom of a large saucepan half-filled with boiling water. Carefully lower pudding into saucepan making sure the water comes two-thirds of the way up the sides of basin. Cover and cook for 5 hours, making sure water is constantly bubbling. Check water level from time to time. Remove from saucepan. Leave until cold. Wrap well and store in refrigerator until ready to use. Steam for a further 2 hours before serving. Serve with Brandy Custard.
Serves 6.

Christmas Pudding (Top right)
Brandy Custard (Left)

BRANDY CUSTARD

3 tablespoons Edmonds custard powder
2 tablespoons sugar
1½ cups milk
1 tablespoon butter
2 tablespoons brandy or rum
pinch of nutmeg

In a saucepan, mix custard powder, sugar and ¼ cup of the milk to a smooth paste. Add remaining milk. Stir over a low heat until mixture thickens and comes to the boil. Remove from heat. Stir in butter, brandy and nutmeg.
Makes 1½ cups.

ORANGE MARINATED STRAWBERRIES

¼ cup thinly pared orange zest
1 cup freshly squeezed orange juice
¼ cup sugar
1 large chip or 400 g strawberries

Cut orange zest into thin strips. Place orange zest, juice and sugar in a saucepan. Bring to the boil and simmer for 5 minutes. Leave to cool. Hull strawberries and cut in half. Place in a bowl. Pour over orange mixture. Leave to marinate for 2 hours at room temperature or overnight in the refrigerator, mixing regularly. Serve lightly chilled.
Serves 4.

FESTIVE TIRAMISU TERRINE

3 teaspoons instant coffee
¾ cup boiling water
¼ cup brandy
250 g packet sponge fingers
(savoiardi biscuits)
100 g dark chocolate, chopped
(or bits or melts)

300 ml cream
1 teaspoon gelatine
1 tablespoon cold water
¼ cup icing sugar
300 g mascarpone cheese
10–12 whole strawberries, hulled

Dissolve coffee in boiling water. Stir in brandy. Line a 21 cm x 11 cm loaf tin with plastic wrap so that it extends over the side of the tin. One by one, quickly dip 8 biscuits into the coffee mixture. Line the base of the tin with the biscuits. Keep remaining coffee mixture. Combine chocolate and ¼ cup of the cream in the top of a double boiler or heatproof bowl. Place over simmering water. Stir constantly until chocolate melts and the mixture is smooth. Remove from heat. Sprinkle gelatine over cold water. Place over a bowl of hot water and stir until gelatine dissolves. Stir into chocolate. Whip remaining cream and icing sugar together. Place mascarpone in a medium bowl. Beat with a wooden spoon until smooth. Fold in cream and chocolate. Spoon half the mixture evenly over biscuits. Place the strawberries in a line down the middle of the chocolate mixture. Carefully spoon over remaining chocolate mixture. Dip 9 more biscuits in reserved coffee mixture. Arrange on top of chocolate layer to cover completely. Fold plastic wrap over the terrine. Refrigerate for 4 hours. To serve, unfold plastic wrap from the top of the terrine. Invert onto a board or flat surface. Using a sharp knife, cut into slices.
Serves 6–8.

INDIVIDUAL BAKED ALASKAS

ICE CREAM
½ cup blanched almonds,
toasted and chopped
¼ cup raisins
¼ cup red cherries, chopped
2 tablespoons chopped
mixed peel
¼ cup dark rum
3 eggs, at room temperature

¼ cup caster sugar
300 ml cream, whipped

MERINGUE
3 egg whites, at room
temperature
½ cup caster sugar
½ teaspoon vanilla essence

To make the Ice Cream, combine almonds, dried fruit and rum in a bowl. Set aside for 30 minutes. Separate eggs. Using an electric mixer, beat egg yolks for 2–3 minutes. Gradually add caster sugar, beating until thick and pale. Fold in cream. Beat egg whites until stiff but not dry. Fold into yolk mixture. Lastly, fold in fruit mixture. Divide between six 1-cup capacity teacups. Cover and freeze for at least 4 hours. Working quickly, remove ice cream from cups by dipping them quickly into hot water, then inverting onto an oven tray. Cover and return to the freezer for 1 hour. To make the Meringue, beat egg whites to a soft foam. Gradually add caster sugar, beating continuously. Add essence and beat until meringue is thick and glossy. Cover ice cream moulds with the meringue, peaking it slightly – the ice cream must be completely covered with meringue or it will melt when baked. Return Alaskas to the freezer for 15 minutes. Bake at 250°C for about 2 minutes until the meringue peaks are golden. Serve immediately.

PAVLOVA

4 egg whites
1½ cups caster sugar
1 teaspoon DYC white vinegar
1 teaspoon vanilla essence
1 tablespoon Edmonds Fielder's cornflour
whipped cream
fresh berries and mint leaves to garnish

Preheat oven to 180°C. Using an electric mixer, beat egg whites and caster sugar for 10–15 minutes or until thick and glossy. Mix vinegar, essence and cornflour together. Add to meringue. Beat on high speed for a further 5 minutes. Line an oven tray with baking paper. Draw a 22 cm circle on the baking paper. Spread the pavlova to within 2 cm of the edge of the circle, keeping the shape as round and even as possible. Smooth top surface. Place pavlova in preheated oven then turn oven temperature down to 100°C. Bake pavlova for 1 hour. Turn off oven. Open oven door slightly and leave pavlova in oven until cold. Carefully lift pavlova onto a serving plate. Decorate with whipped cream, fresh berries and mint leaves.
Serves 6.

SHERRY TRIFLE

4 tablespoons Edmonds custard powder

3 tablespoons sugar

2 cups milk

2 egg whites

200 g trifle sponge

¼ cup raspberry or apricot jam

¼ cup sherry

410 g can fruit salad

¾ cup cream

2 teaspoons icing sugar

¼ cup toasted slivered almonds to decorate

To make the custard, mix custard powder, sugar and ¼ cup of the milk to a smooth paste in a saucepan. Add remaining milk and stir over a low heat until mixture comes to the boil. Simmer for 2–3 minutes or until custard thickens, stirring constantly. Remove from heat, cover and leave until cold. When custard has cooled, beat egg whites until stiff. Fold custard into egg whites. Cut sponge in half horizontally. Spread cut surface with jam. Sandwich halves together. Cut into cubes then arrange in 6 individual serving dishes or 1 large serving bowl. Spoon sherry over sponge. Spoon fruit salad and juice evenly over sponge. Spoon custard over fruit salad. Chill until set. Beat cream and icing sugar until thick. Decorate trifles with cream and almonds.

N.B. To speed up the cooling of the custard, transfer mixture from the saucepan to a heatproof bowl. Stand in a bowl of iced water.

Serves 6.

SUMMER PUDDING

5 cups mixed berry fruit
1¼ cups sugar
10 slices stale toast-cut bread
8–10 fresh berries to garnish

Prepare fruit by washing, drying, hulling and slicing if large. Mix fruit and sugar together in a saucepan and heat gently until almost boiling. Remove from heat. Cool. Remove ¼ cup of berry juice and set aside. Cut crusts from bread and cut each slice into 3 fingers. Arrange bread around the inside of a 6-cup-capacity pudding basin. Spoon in one-third of the berry mixture. Layer with more bread and fruit. Repeat layers once more, finishing with a layer of bread. Spoon over enough berry juice to moisten bread. Cover with plastic wrap and weigh down with a heavy weight. Refrigerate for at least 2 hours or overnight. Turn onto a serving plate. Brush reserved juice over any sections of bread not soaked with juice. Garnish pudding with fresh berries.
Serves 6–8.

CHRISTMAS COOKIES

125 g butter, softened
¾ cup caster sugar
1 egg
1 teaspoon vanilla essence
2 cups Champion standard grade flour
½ teaspoon Edmonds baking powder
¼ cup cocoa
narrow ribbon to hang biscuits

Cream butter and sugar until light and fluffy. Add egg. Beat well. Beat in essence. Sift flour, baking powder and cocoa. Stir into creamed mixture, mixing to a soft dough. Shape dough into a ball. Cover with plastic wrap and refrigerate for 30 minutes. Roll dough out on a floured surface to a thickness of 5 mm. Using Christmas-shaped biscuit cutters, stamp out shapes. Place on greased oven trays. Using a metal or wooden skewer, make a small hole in the top of each biscuit. Bake at 180°C for 12 minutes. Cool on wire racks. To hang the biscuits from the Christmas tree, thread ribbon through the hole in the top of each biscuit, tying the ends together.

N.B. The biscuits will not stay fresh for longer than 1 day hanging from the tree.

Christmas Mince Pies (Top right)
Christmas Cookies (Left)
Christmas Mincemeat (Right)

CHRISTMAS MINCEMEAT

1¼ cups currants

1¼ cups sultanas

1¼ cups raisins

1¼ cups mixed peel

¼ cup blanched almonds

2 medium apples, unpeeled, quartered and cored

1 cup brown sugar

¼ teaspoon salt

½ teaspoon ground nutmeg

2 tablespoons brandy or whisky or lemon juice

Mince or finely chop currants, sultanas, raisins, peel and almonds. Finely chop or grate apples. Add apples, sugar, salt, nutmeg and brandy to fruit mixture. Mix well. Cover and refrigerate. Stir occasionally. Christmas Mincemeat will keep for up to 3 months in the refrigerator.

Makes 6 cups.

CHRISTMAS MINCE PIES

SWEET SHORTCRUST PASTRY
(or 400 g purchased sweet
shortcrust pastry)
1 cup Champion standard
grade flour
75 g butter
¼ cup sugar

1 egg yolk
1 tablespoon cold water
1 cup Christmas Mincemeat
(see page 38)
1 egg, beaten
icing sugar to dust

To make the pastry, sift flour. Cut in butter until it resembles fine breadcrumbs. Stir in sugar. Add egg yolk and water. Mix to a stiff dough. Chill for 30 minutes before using. On a lightly floured board, roll out pastry to 3 mm thickness. Cut out rounds using a 7 cm cutter, and use to line about 16 patty tins. Using a 6 cm round biscuit cutter, cut out tops from the remaining pastry. Spoon teaspoons of Christmas Mincemeat into each base. Brush the edges of the bases with some of the egg. Place tops over the filling, pressing lightly around the edges to seal the pies. Glaze with the remaining beaten egg. Bake at 180°C for 15 minutes or until golden. To serve, heat at 140°C for 15 minutes or until warm. Dust with icing sugar.
Makes 16.

FLORENTINES

125 g butter, softened
½ cup sugar
5 tablespoons golden syrup
¼ cup Champion standard grade flour
70 g packet sliced almonds
½ cup chopped glacé cherries
½ cup chopped walnuts
¼ cup chopped mixed peel
150 g cooking chocolate, melted

Cream butter and sugar. Beat in syrup. Sift in flour. Add almonds, cherries, walnuts and peel. Mix well. Place level tablespoons of mixture on trays lined with baking paper, spacing them well apart to allow for spreading. Cook four at a time. Press each one out as flat and round as possible, using a knife. Bake in the oven at 180°C for 10 minutes or until golden brown. Remove from oven and leave on tray for 5 minutes before transferring to a wire rack. When cold spread melted chocolate on the flat side of each biscuit.
Makes 24.

Meringues (Top)
Florentines (Left)
Tiny Lemon Curd Tartlets (Right)

MERINGUES

2 egg whites
½ cup caster sugar
whipped cream

Using an electric mixer, beat egg whites until stiff but not dry. Add half the sugar and beat well. Repeat with remaining sugar. Pipe or spoon small amounts of meringue onto a greased oven tray. Bake at 120°C for 1–1½ hours or until the meringues are dry but not brown. Cool. Store unfilled meringues in an airtight container. To serve, sandwich together with whipped cream or serve as an accompaniment to fresh fruit salad and whipped cream.
Makes 18.

TINY LEMON CURD TARTLETS

LEMON CURD FILLING
1 tablespoon finely grated
lemon zest
¼ cup lemon juice
2 eggs, lightly beaten
50 g butter
¼ cup caster sugar

PASTRY
100 g butter, softened
¼ cup caster sugar
1 egg yolk
1 cup Champion standard
grade flour

To make the Lemon Curd Filling, combine lemon zest and juice, eggs, butter and sugar in the top of a double boiler or in a heatproof bowl. Place over simmering water. Stir constantly until sugar dissolves and curd thickens. Remove from heat. Cover and cool.

For the Pastry, cream butter and sugar until light and fluffy. Add egg yolk and beat well. Stir in flour. Gather pastry into a ball and wrap in plastic wrap. Refrigerate for 20 minutes. Roll pastry out on a lightly floured surface to a thickness of 2–3 mm. Using a 7 cm round biscuit cutter, cut circles from pastry. Transfer to deep mini muffin tins. Prick bases with a fork. Freeze for 5 minutes. Bake at 180°C for 10 minutes until golden. Remove pastry cases from tins and cool on a wire rack. Just before serving, fill with lemon curd.

Makes 24 tartlets.

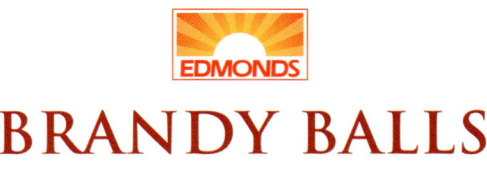

BRANDY BALLS

250 g packet Vanilla Wine biscuits
2 tablespoons currants
2 tablespoons chopped walnuts
1 egg
¼ cup sugar
1 tablespoon cocoa
1½ tablespoons brandy or sherry
125 g butter, melted
coconut or chocolate hail

Finely crush biscuits. Combine biscuit crumbs, currants and walnuts in a bowl. In another bowl lightly beat the egg with a fork. Add sugar and cocoa, stirring until thoroughly mixed. Add brandy. Pour into crumb mixture. Add melted butter. Stir until well combined. Measure level tablespoons of mixture and shape into balls. Roll in coconut or chocolate hail. Chill until firm.
Makes about 26.

RUM BALLS
Add 1½ tablespoons of rum in place of the brandy.

Chocolate Fudge (Top right)
Coconut Ice (Left)
Brandy Balls (Right)

CHOCOLATE FUDGE

2 cups sugar
2 tablespoons cocoa
½ cup milk
25 g butter
½ teaspoon vanilla essence
½ cup chopped walnuts (optional)

Put sugar and cocoa into a saucepan. Mix to combine. Add milk and butter. Heat gently, stirring constantly until sugar has dissolved and butter has melted. Bring to the boil. Do not stir. Let mixture boil until the soft ball stage. To test for soft ball stage, drop a small amount of mixture off a teaspoon into cold water. When a soft ball forms, the mixture is ready. On a sugar thermometer, the soft ball stage is 116°C. Remove from heat. Add essence and leave to stand for 5 minutes. Stir in walnuts. Beat with a wooden spoon until thick. Pour into a buttered tin. Mark into squares. Cut when cold.

COCONUT ICE

4 cups icing sugar
½ cup milk
2 tablespoons butter
¼ teaspoon salt

1 cup coconut
few drops of red food
colouring (optional)

Put icing sugar, milk, butter and salt into a saucepan. Heat gently, stirring constantly until sugar dissolves. Bring to the boil. Do not stir. Let mixture boil until the soft ball stage. To test for soft ball stage, drop a small amount of mixture off a teaspoon into cold water. When a soft ball forms, the mixture is ready. On a sugar thermometer, the soft ball stage is 116°C. Add coconut. Remove from heat and allow to cool for 10 minutes. Beat until mixture starts to thicken. Pour into a buttered tin. Allow to cool. Cut into squares.

N.B. If desired, divide the mixture in half before beating and add a few drops of red food colouring to one portion. Beat the white portion until it starts to thicken. Spread this mixture on top of pink mixture.

YULETIDE CARAMELS

2½ cups sugar
2 tablespoons coconut
1 teaspoon ground ginger
1 tablespoon golden syrup

25 g butter
½ cup milk
1 teaspoon vanilla essence

Put sugar, coconut and ginger into a saucepan. Mix to combine. Add golden syrup, butter and milk. Heat gently, stirring constantly until sugar dissolves. Bring to the boil. Do not stir. Boil mixture until soft ball stage. To test for soft ball stage, drop a small amount of mixture off a teaspoon into cold water. When a soft ball forms, the mixture is ready. On a sugar thermometer, this is 116°C. Remove from heat. Add essence and beat until thick and creamy. Pour into a buttered tin. Mark into squares. Cut when cold.

RUSSIAN FUDGE

3 cups sugar
½ cup milk
½ cup sweetened condensed milk

125 g butter
⅛ teaspoon salt
1 tablespoon golden syrup

Put sugar and milk into a saucepan. Heat gently, stirring constantly until sugar dissolves. Add condensed milk, butter, salt and golden syrup. Stir until butter has melted. Bring to the boil and continue boiling to the soft ball stage, stirring occasionally to prevent burning. To test for soft ball stage, drop a small amount of mixture off a teaspoon into cold water. When a soft ball forms, the mixture is ready. On a sugar thermometer, the soft ball stage is 116°C. Remove from heat. Cool slightly. Beat until thick. Pour into a buttered tin. Mark into squares. Cut when cold.

N.B. Vanilla essence or chopped nuts may be added to fudge before beating.

Stained Glass Window Log (Top), Yuletide Caramels (Second from top), Hazelnut Chocolate Truffles (Third from top), Russian Fudge (Bottom)

STAINED GLASS WINDOW LOG

¾ cup brazil nuts, toasted and roughly chopped
10 red glace cherries, halved
10 green glace cherries, halved
12 dried apricots, quartered
250 g dark chocolate, roughly chopped (or melts or bits)
½ cup sweetened condensed milk
3 tablespoons cream

Combine nuts and dried fruit in a bowl. Place chocolate, condensed milk and cream in the top of a double boiler or heatproof bowl. Place over simmering water and stir constantly until chocolate melts and mixture is smooth. Remove from heat. Add nut and fruit mixture. Mix well. Lay a 45 cm length of foil on a flat surface. Transfer chocolate mixture to the centre of the foil. Fold the foil over the mixture, then roll into a log about 35 cm long. Twist the ends of the foil to enclose the log. Refrigerate for 3–4 hours until firm. To serve, cut into slices. Store in the refrigerator.

HAZELNUT CHOCOLATE TRUFFLES

250 g dark chocolate, chopped (or melts or bits)
25 g butter, chopped
½ cup cream
1 tablespoon Frangelico liqueur (optional)
¼ cup ground roasted hazelnuts
200 g dark chocolate, chopped (or melts or bits)
21 hazelnuts, halved, to garnish

Place chocolate and butter in the top of a double boiler or heatproof bowl. Place over simmering water. Stir constantly until chocolate melts and the mixture is smooth. Remove from heat. Stir in cream, liqueur and ground hazelnuts. Cover and refrigerate for several hours until firm. Roll teaspoons of mixture into balls. Place in a single layer on a plate. Cover with plastic wrap and refrigerate for 1 hour. To coat truffles, melt second measure of chocolate as above. Cool slightly. Quickly dip truffles into the melted chocolate using a dipping stick or teaspoons. Allow excess chocolate to drain off. Place on a sheet of foil. Garnish each truffle with half a hazelnut. Allow to dry before storing in a covered container in a cool place.
Makes 42 truffles.

DRIED FRUIT COMPOTE

2 cups freshly squeezed orange juice (about 8 oranges)

½ cup water

⅓ cup runny honey

2 cinnamon sticks

⅓ cup brandy

200 g dried apricots

150 g dried figs

100 g pitted prunes

Strain orange juice through a fine sieve into a saucepan. Add water, honey and one cinnamon stick. Stir over a low heat until honey dissolves. Bring to the boil, reduce heat and simmer for 45 minutes. Remove cinnamon stick and discard. Stir in brandy. Pack dried fruit and remaining cinnamon stick into a clean sterilised jar. Pour syrup over fruit. Cover jar tightly with a lid. Cool. Store in the refrigerator. Serve with whipped cream, ice cream or yoghurt.

PANETTONE

1 teaspoon sugar
¼ cup warm water
4 teaspoons Edmonds active yeast
¾ cup milk
75 g butter
4 cups Champion high grade flour
⅓ cup sugar

½ teaspoon salt
4 egg yolks, lightly beaten
¾ cup sultanas
¼ cup mixed peel
finely grated zest of 1 lemon
milk to brush

Dissolve first measure of sugar in warm water. Sprinkle yeast over water. Set aside in a warm place for 10 minutes until frothy. Place milk and butter in a small saucepan. Stir over a low heat until butter melts. Transfer to a large bowl and allow to cool to lukewarm. Stir in frothy yeast mixture. Using a wooden spoon beat in 1 cup of the flour, and the sugar and salt. Cover with plastic wrap and stand in a warm place until mixture is bubbly. Mix yolks and remaining flour into the yeast mixture. Add sultanas, mixed peel and lemon zest. Mix to a soft dough with a wooden spoon. Turn dough onto a floured surface and knead for 10 minutes until smooth and elastic. Place dough in a lightly oiled bowl, turning to coat with oil. Cover with plastic wrap. Stand in a warm place until doubled in bulk (about 1½ hours). Punch dough down with a fist, then knead for 1 minute on a lightly floured surface. Form into a large ball and place in a greased, deep, 20 cm round cake tin that has been lined with baking paper on the base. Cover with plastic wrap and stand in a warm place until doubled in bulk. Brush top of Panettone with milk. Bake in the lower third of the oven at 200°C for 15 minutes, then reduce heat to 180°C and bake for a further 30 minutes or until bread sounds hollow when tapped. Leave in tin for 10 minutes before transferring to a wire rack to cool. To serve, cut into wedges. Serve buttered.

N.B. Panettone is best eaten on the day it is made, however it will keep for up to 4 days. It is delicious toasted.

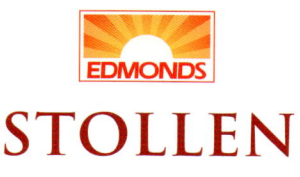

STOLLEN

1 teaspoon sugar
¼ cup tepid water
1 tablespoon Edmonds active yeast
¾ cup milk
¼ cup sugar
100 g butter
½ teaspoon salt
3½ cups Champion high grade flour

1 egg
2 cups mixed dried fruit
½ cup toasted almonds
¼ cup brandy
200 g marzipan
melted butter
icing sugar to dust

Dissolve first measure of sugar in water. Sprinkle over yeast. Set aside until frothy. Heat milk, second measure of sugar, butter and salt together. Cool. Add yeast to milk mixture. Beat 1 cup of the flour into milk mixture with a wooden spoon. Cover and set aside in a warm place until batter is bubbly. Beat egg and mix into batter with remaining flour. Mix dried fruit, almonds and brandy together. Mix into dough. Turn onto a lightly floured board and knead until smooth and elastic. Place in a greased bowl. Turn dough over and cover with plastic wrap. Set aside in a warm place until double in bulk. Punch dough down and knead lightly. Shape dough into a 20 x 30 cm rectangle on a greased oven tray. Roll marzipan into a 30 cm roll. Place marzipan one-third of the way from the dough's long edge. Fold the remaining two-thirds of the rectangle over the marzipan to within 5 cm of the long edge. Brush with melted butter. Cover with a clean cloth. Set aside in a warm place until double in bulk. If preferred, cut the mixture in half and make two smaller stollen. Bake at 200°C for 15 minutes. Reduce heat to 180°C and cook for 15 minutes or until stollen sounds hollow when tapped. Cool and dust with icing sugar.

Stollen (Top left)
Panforte (Top right)
Almond Shortbread Rings (Left)

ALMOND SHORTBREAD RINGS

250 g butter, softened
1 cup icing sugar
3-4 drops almond essence
1½ cups Champion standard grade flour
¾ cup Edmonds Fielder's cornflour
70 g packet ground almonds

Cream butter and icing sugar until light and fluffy. Add essence. Sift flour and cornflour. Stir into butter mixture, along with ground almonds, mixing to a soft dough. Transfer dough to a lightly floured surface. Knead lightly for 2 minutes. Divide dough in half. Shape each portion into a ball and place in the centre of lightly greased oven trays. Pat or roll into a 20 cm round circle. Using a sharp knife or pizza wheel, divide dough into 8 equal portions, cutting almost right through the dough. Prick each section several times with a fork. Bake at 150°C for 40 minutes. Cool on a wire rack. To divide shortbread, break into sections along the marked lines.

PANFORTE

1 cup hazelnuts, toasted
and roughly chopped
1 cup blanched almonds, toasted
and roughly chopped
½ cup dried figs, chopped
½ cup dried apricots, chopped
¼ cup crystallised ginger, chopped

¼ cup mixed peel
¾ cup Champion high grade flour
1 teaspoon cinnamon
¾ teaspoon ground nutmeg
¼ teaspoon ground cloves
½ cup runny honey
½ cup caster sugar

Thoroughly grease a 20 cm round cake tin. Line the base and sides with baking paper. Combine nuts, dried fruit, flour and spices in a mixing bowl. Mix well. Place honey and sugar in a small saucepan. Stir over a low heat until sugar dissolves. Bring to the boil, stirring constantly. Boil for about 2 minutes until mixture reaches the soft ball stage. To test for soft ball stage, drop a small amount of mixture off a teaspoon into cold water. When a soft ball forms, the mixture is ready. On a sugar thermometer, the soft ball stage is 116°C. Do not let the syrup change colour. Remove from the heat and let the bubbles subside. Carefully pour syrup over dry ingredients, then quickly mix to combine. Press into prepared tin. (Speed is vital, as the mixture will become sticky and unmanageable very quickly.) Bake at 150°C for 45 minutes in the lower third of the oven. Cool in tin. Wrap in foil and store in the refrigerator. To serve, cut into thin wedges.

ACKNOWLEDGEMENTS

Tableware kindly supplied by the Studio of Tableware, Mt Eden.

ISBN 1-86958-775-8

© 1999 Original text and photography – Bluebird Foods Ltd
The moral rights of the author have been asserted

© 1999 Design and format – Hodder Moa Beckett Publishers Limited

Published in 1999 by Hodder Moa Beckett Publishers Limited,
[a member of the Hodder Headline Group]
4 Whetu Place, Mairangi Bay, Auckland, New Zealand

Produced and designed by Hodder Moa Beckett Publishers Ltd
Text and food styling by Sue Lyons
Photography by Bruce Benson

Scanning and colour separations by Microdot, Auckland.
Printed by Kyodo Printing Co. Ltd, Singapore